NATURE'S GIANTS

ELEPHANTS

BY MARISSA KIRKMAN

WWW.APEXEDITIONS.COM

Apex is distributed by North Star Editions:
sales@northstareditions.com | 888-417-0195

Produced for Apex by Red Line Editorial.

Photographs ©: Shutterstock Images, cover, 1, 4–5, 6, 7, 8–9, 10–11, 12, 13, 14–15, 16–17, 18, 19, 20, 22–23, 24, 25, 29; iStockphoto, 26–27

Library of Congress Control Number: 2023921577

ISBN
978-1-63738-934-8 (hardcover)
978-1-63738-974-4 (paperback)
979-8-89250-068-5 (ebook pdf)
979-8-89250-032-6 (hosted ebook)

Printed in the United States of America
Mankato, MN
082024

NOTE TO PARENTS AND EDUCATORS

Apex books are designed to build literacy skills in striving readers. Exciting, high-interest content attracts and holds readers' attention. The text is carefully leveled to allow students to achieve success quickly. Additional features, such as bolded glossary words for difficult terms, help build comprehension.

TABLE OF CONTENTS

CHAPTER 1

LARGEST LAND ANIMAL

An elephant marches across the **savanna**. The hot sun warms the animal's skin. It flaps its big ears to cool down.

An elephant's ears help release heat from its body.

Elephants can smell water under the ground. They dig to reach it.

The elephant stomps its foot on the dry ground. It uses its **tusks** to dig through the dirt. Soon it finds water hidden underground.

LONG TEETH

Most elephants grow two long tusks. They use these teeth to dig, fight, and move things. A male elephant's tusks can weigh more than 220 pounds (100 kg).

Male elephants use their tusks to fight over mates.

The elephant sucks up water with its trunk. It sprays the water into its mouth. Then the giant animal goes to look for food.

FAST FACT

Elephants are the largest land **mammals** on Earth.

An elephant can hold up to 2.6 gallons (10 L) of water in its trunk.

CHAPTER 2

THREE TYPES

There are three **species** of elephants. African bush elephants are the largest. They stand up to 13 feet (4 m) tall. And they can weigh more than 12,000 pounds (5,440 kg).

African bush elephants live in forests and grasslands throughout much of Africa.

African forest elephants are smaller. They can grow 10 feet tall (3 m) and weigh about 10,000 pounds (4,540 kg).

African forest elephants live in thick rainforests.

The tusks of African forest elephants are straight and point down.

FAST FACT

African forest elephants have bigger ears and longer trunks than bush elephants.

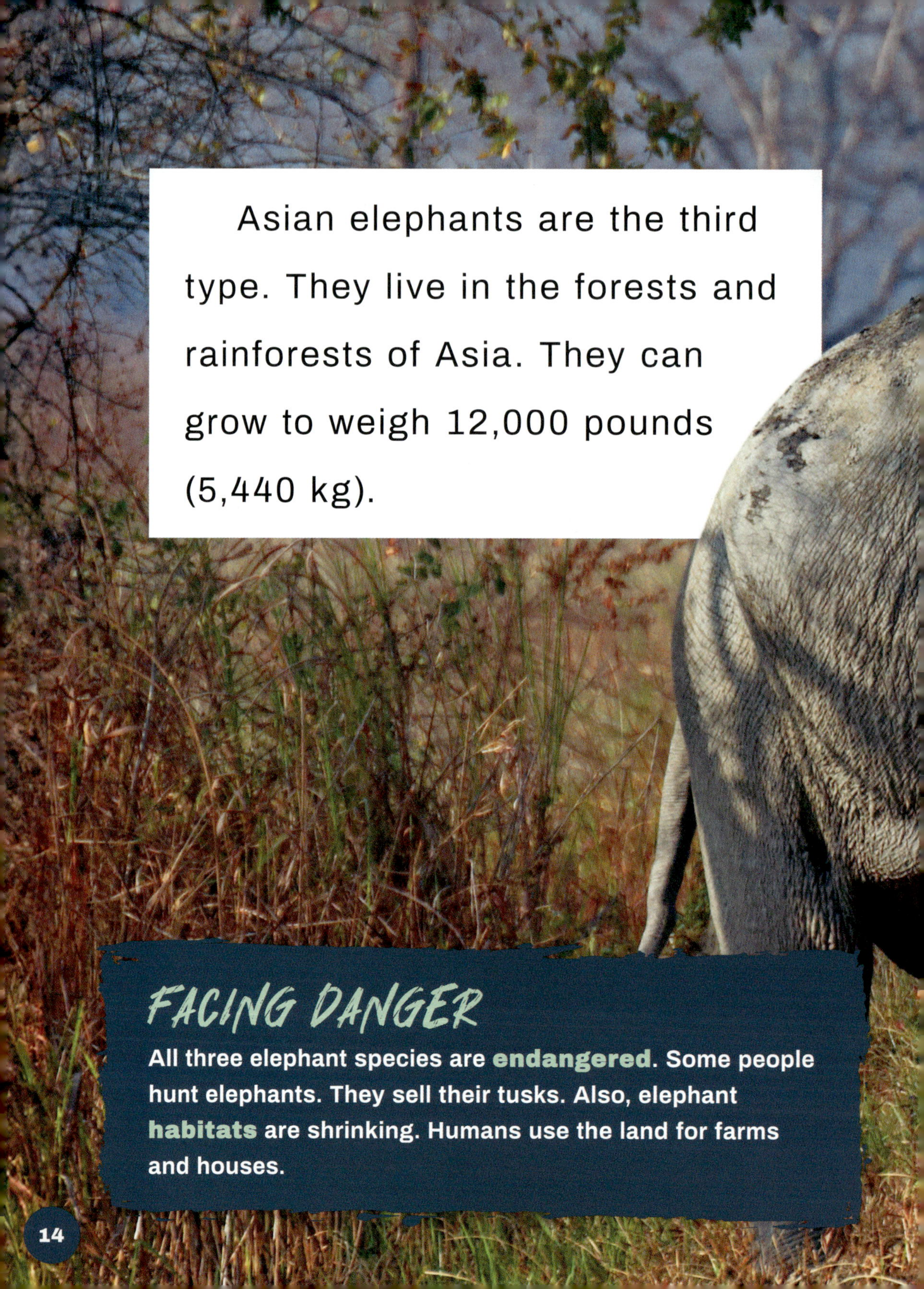

Asian elephants are the third type. They live in the forests and rainforests of Asia. They can grow to weigh 12,000 pounds (5,440 kg).

FACING DANGER

All three elephant species are **endangered**. Some people hunt elephants. They sell their tusks. Also, elephant **habitats** are shrinking. Humans use the land for farms and houses.

Asian elephants have rounder and smaller ears than other types of elephants.

CHAPTER 3

LIFE IN THE WILD

Elephants eat plants. They often eat grass, fruits, and leaves. They use their long trunks to grab food.

Elephants can reach high into trees to get food.

Elephants spend about 16 hours eating each day.

Elephants spend lots of time looking for food. They can eat 350 pounds (160 kg) of food each day. And they can drink up to 50 gallons (190 L) of water.

A MIGHTY TRUNK

The trunk is part of an elephant's top lip and nose. It has many muscles. As a result, it is strong and flexible. It can bend and grip things. An elephant can even use it to pull down trees.

Elephants are strong swimmers. They hold their trunks above the water to breathe.

Elephants also **migrate** each year. They leave dry places to find food and water. Some travel more than 60 miles (100 km).

FAST FACT

Elephants have large brains and good memories. They go back to places where they found water in the past.

◀ Elephants may travel in large groups when they migrate.

CHAPTER 4

HUGE HERD

Elephants live in groups called herds. Each herd includes many females and their babies. The oldest female is the leader.

One herd can have as many as 100 elephants.

Elephants may stand in a circle around calves to keep them safe.

Female elephants have one calf about every four years. All the elephants in a herd work together to care for the babies.

COMMUNICATING

Elephants **communicate** in many ways. They make trumpeting sounds with their trunks. They tap or shake trunks to greet one another. Elephants may flap their ears to show feelings as well.

Elephants may trumpet when they're excited, happy, or scared.

FAST FACT

An elephant can live for 70 years.

By age 13, elephants are fully grown. At that time, males go off to live on their own. Females typically stay with the same herd for life.

Male elephants are called bulls. Females are called cows.

COMPREHENSION QUESTIONS

Write your answers on a separate piece of paper.

1. Write a sentence that explains the main idea of Chapter 2.

2. Would you rather live in a savanna or a rainforest? Why?

3. How many species of elephants are there?

   A. one
   B. two
   C. three

4. Which type of elephant is the smallest?

   A. African forest elephant
   B. African bush elephant
   C. Asian elephant

5. What does **flexible** mean in this book?

*As a result, it is strong and **flexible**. It can bend and grip things.*

A. needing to hold very still
B. able to make lots of noise
C. able to move, twist, or bend

6. What does **includes** mean in this book?

*Elephants live in groups called herds. Each herd **includes** many females and their babies.*

A. is made up of
B. keeps separate
C. looks for

Answer key on page 32.

GLOSSARY

communicate

To send and receive messages.

endangered

In danger of dying out forever.

habitats

The places where animals normally live.

mammals

Animals that have hair and produce milk for their young.

migrate

To move from one part of the world to another.

savanna

A flat, grassy area with few or no trees.

species

Groups of animals or plants that are similar and can breed with one another.

tusks

Long teeth that stick out of an animal's mouth.

TO LEARN MORE

BOOKS

Duling, Kaitlyn. *African Elephants.* Minneapolis: Bellwether Media, 2020.

Grodzicki, Jenna. *Elephant.* Minneapolis: Bearport Publishing, 2022.

Sang, Maivboon. *Elephant Cows: Heads of the Herd.* North Mankato, MN: Capstone, 2023.

ONLINE RESOURCES

Visit **www.apexeditions.com** to find links and resources related to this title.

ABOUT THE AUTHOR

Marissa Kirkman is a writer and editor who lives in Illinois. She enjoys reading about animals, science, and history.

INDEX

ANSWER KEY:
1. Answers will vary; 2. Answers will vary; 3. C; 4. A; 5. C; 6. A